Ten

for Authors

Simple writing strategies
and creative writing prompts
for authors!

Jed Jurchenko

Coffee Shop
CONVERSATIONS

www.CoffeeShopConversations.com

© 2019 by Jed Jurchenko.

Printed by KDP,
An Amazon.com Company
Available from Amazon.com

Dedicated to writers
who love to write and who strive
to make the world a better place,
one book, article, and blog post at a time.

Also by Jed

Ten Quick Wins for Writers

131 Conversations That Engage Kids

131 Boredom Busters and Creativity Builders

131 Creative Conversations for Couples

131 Engaging Conversations for Couples

131 Creative Conversations for Families

131 Necessary Conversations before Marriage

131 Conversations for Stepfamily Success

131 Connecting Conversations
for Parents and Teens

Coffee Shop Conversations:
Psychology and the Bible

Get Free Books!

Thank you for purchasing this book! I would love to send you a free bonus gift.

Transform from discouraged and burned out to an enthusiastic agent of joy who leads at a higher, happier level! *Be Happier Now* is easy to apply and is perfect for parents, stepparents, mentors, pastors, coaches, and friends.

Discover practical strategies for staying energized so you can encourage and refresh others. This easy-to-read book will guide you each step of the way!

Yes, send me *Be Happier Now!*
www.coffeeshopconversations.com/happiness

Contents

131 Writing Prompts for Action Takers......77

Motivation for Massive Writing Action....108

***

Chasing the Writing Dream

What if you are just one great idea away from building massive momentum and achieving your writing dreams? At this moment, you may be suffering from a severe case of writer's block. Perhaps a fear of failure or rejection holds you back. Maybe you long to write a book but have no idea where to start. If any of these statements apply to you, don't fret. Instead, know that you could be one great idea away from your breakthrough!

I know because I experience the power of ideas firsthand. I often get stuck. At times, I am paralyzed by self-doubt, fear of failure, and the dread of personal rejection. For a long time, I wasn't disciplined enough to write consistently, and I had no clue how to get published. Happily, today, I also know the thrill of overcoming each of these barriers. As a result, I am able to share my message with more people than I ever imagined possible!

This same opportunity is available to you. Right now, you can begin writing your book — or many books, if you wish. Not only will publishing a book allow you to impact the lives of people all over the globe, but book sales can also become a steady source of income for your family. For some authors, a book opens the door to new speaking engagements. Other authors build online courses and offer personalized coaching to help readers dive deeper into their book's content. Some writers even use their book to fashion their career around their true calling. I believe all of this is possible, as long as you have an idea and are willing to act.

In *Rich Dad Poor Dad,* Robert Kiyosaki writes, "Every self-made person started small with an idea, and then turned it into something big."[1] This statement is equally true for authors. Every writing breakthrough begins with an idea, which is why I firmly believe you are just one great idea away from writing success.

Finding Your Breakthrough

For years I longed to write a book. Sadly, I got stuck in a vicious cycle of writing, getting distracted, restarting, becoming distracted again, and then giving up. After multiple failures, I felt lost. Then, a simple idea gave me a clear path to follow and ignited a sequence of writing successes.

Welcome to *Ten Great Ideas for Authors.* This book has three simple yet crucial goals. The first is to help you grow as a writer. One great idea helped me transform from frustrated and stuck into a steadfast writer. I believe that you are one great idea away from your breakthrough, too.

This is my eighteenth book, and I plan to publish many more. In the pages ahead, I am excited to introduce you to ten of the best writing ideas I know. These strategies will help you develop a consistent writing habit, engage your readers, and courageously share your message with the world.

My second goal is to help you put these ideas into practice. Great ideas are only effective when acted upon, which means ongoing practice is a must. It is estimated that 80 percent of adults long to write a book, but only a small percentage of them ever achieve this goal.[2] The ones who make it are the action takers. Today, the publishing industry's doors are wide open. With the rise of self-publishing, anyone with a computer and a message can publish a book.

In fact, last year I had the privilege of helping my ten-year-old daughter, Brooklyn, finish her book. Watching Brooklyn's face light up as she shared her story with teachers, classmates, family, and friends was a highlight of my year. After publishing, Brooklyn received an email from a kind librarian who purchased her book, added it to the school's collection, and began telling kids that if they want it badly enough, they can be a published author too. I love how my daughter is inspiring other children to pursue their dreams.

If you are part of the masses who desire to publish but keep getting stuck, then these ideas are for you. Although I have included ten of them, just one great idea may be enough. Your job is to find the right one and put it into practice.

Finally, the third goal of this book is to inspire you to move from occasional practice to taking massive action. Writers write! This simple idea changed my life. I'll tell you more about it in chapter three. For now, know that this theme is woven throughout the book and ties each section together. Because taking action is a must, chapter four contains 131 creative writing prompts. These prompts will help you jumpstart your imagination and build momentum fast.

Ideas and action cannot be separated. If ideas are the ignition button that causes the rocket to blast off, then taking action is the fuel that will propel you to new heights. Action is necessary because all books are written in exactly the same way, one word at a time. As a writer, your primary job is to get your message out of your head and onto paper. Just know, developing a daily writing routine is far easier said than done.

In the pages ahead, I share the ideas that work for me. I also provide ample opportunities to put them into practice. Lastly, I encourage you to take massive action while cheering you on every step of the way. I hope this book helps you find your idea or ideas quickly and reignite your writing dreams!

Idea Stacking

"So, what can you do to earn an extra $800 a month?" my friend Eric asked for the third time. *Man, is he persistent,* I thought to myself. My shoulders tensed in frustration. This was not the pity party I had hoped for. My inner toddler wanted to toss my cellphone across the park in a fit of infantile rage.

Instead, I forced a more mature side of me to assume control. After taking a deep breath and composing myself, I dully replied, "I guess I could write more." Fortunately, my lack of enthusiasm did not detour Eric. Eric is my accountability partner and friend. He is also the author of the book *The Best Advice So Far*.[3] As you might imagine, Eric is full of excellent advice.

I called Eric shortly after receiving some nerve-wracking news. The weight of the burden felt like a baby elephant had jumped on my back and asked for a piggyback ride. I wanted to wallow in my newfound misery, but Eric had different plans.

The timing of our bad news could not have been worse. My wife, Jenny, was in her third trimester of pregnancy. The two of us were eagerly anticipating the arrival of our fourth daughter, and our family was on a tight budget. At the time, we lived in San Diego, a pricy city, where the cost of living is roughly 13 percent higher than the national average.

After months of cutting spending, taking on additional jobs, and following a meticulous financial plan, it felt like we were on the right track. Jenny and I knew that once baby Emmalyn arrived, money would be tight. However, we also felt capable of balancing our delicate budget. Then we were hit with a new, major expense. In an instant, all our plans unraveled.

Financially, our family was on a sinking ship, and the size of the bill meant we were taking on water fast. I had been through bankruptcy before, and I had no desire to repeat the process. Internally, I was frightened and frustrated. I wanted Eric to partner with me in shaking my fist at the world. Instead, he insisted on helping me find new ideas.

Today, I am grateful for Eric's persistence. He pushed me when I needed it most, which is precisely what a good friend does. Although I presented my idea with lackluster enthusiasm, Eric acted as if my plan was pure genius. His enthusiasm was contagious. Soon, I doubled my writing efforts, which became the first step in finding our solution.

Idea Stacking

While one great idea can change everything, there are also times when a single idea is not enough. This is where idea stacking comes into play. In 2016, I set out to live every author's dream. I was going to write and publish, write and publish, and then write some more.

I set my alarm for 4 a.m. This way, I could write before my family awoke. I wrote on my smartphone while putting our two-year-old daughter down for naps. I took my laptop to our older girls' soccer practice and wrote in the car while they ran through drills. This focused intensity allowed me to publish several books quickly. The only problem was that each book sat quietly on the digital shelf, with only a few sales each month.

Something New

I heard it said that you and I only have three options. First, we can do more of what we already know does not work. Second, we can do more of what we know works — which is an excellent plan if you have this figured out. Third, we can get innovative and try something new. The idea of increasing my writing output only took me so far. Then I hit a brick wall. It was time to try something new.

One day I came across an advertisement promoting a mastermind community for authors. Because the first month's membership was offered at a discounted rate, I decided to test it out. I planned to gather as many creative ideas from the group as possible and then quietly slip away before the more substantial fees kicked in. However, there was a flaw in my plan. Again, a single idea changed everything. The mastermind group became so valuable I couldn't leave. In fact, I am still a part of it today, as the incredible ideas and ongoing support more than cover the modest charge.

Leadership expert Ken Blanchard says, "None of us is as good as all of us." Teaming up with other experts is powerful because you and I cannot see our own blind spots. If we could, then they wouldn't be blind spots. The idea of increasing my writing output had been a good one. Nevertheless, there was a missing ingredient, and once again, my breakthrough came in the form of an idea.

I asked the leader of our mastermind group, "What can I do to get my books to sell." After pausing for a moment, he thoughtfully replied, "Jed, you can't write, silently publish, and expect your books to sell. The world does not work this way. You need to let everyone know about your books by launching them. Building an engaged book launch team is the best way to get noticed in our noisy world." I let out a sigh of exasperation. I didn't see what difference a launch team would make, and the thought of rallying a team around my book was intimidating.

Nevertheless, he was the expert. I decided following his idea was better than having no idea at all. Little did I know, following this advice would ignite my writing career.

Over the next few months, I discovered I was fully capable of building an encouraging and supportive launch team. Soon, readers began leaving positive reviews. Books which were only selling a few copies a month began selling a few copies a day. I met other writers, which expanded my circle of influence, and launching new books even became fun.

I heard the average book sells roughly 500 copies in its lifetime. Last December I sold well over 4,000 books. For some authors, this is small potatoes. Others would love this kind of momentum. For our family, this was life-changing. Book sales allowed us to balance our budget and patch the hole in our sinking ship. Today, I believe the best is yet to come. I trust this is true for you too.

I share our story because, in this case, it took two great ideas to overcome a significant obstacle. I firmly believe that great ideas can help you push past your barriers. If one idea is not enough, then get innovative and generate a second. Stack your ideas together as you press forward toward your goal. Fran Tarkenton said, "Winning means being unafraid to lose." I like this quote because it affirms that winners don't necessarily get things right the first time.

Often, success follows failure, or at least what we perceive as failure. In my mind, I failed by publishing books that didn't sell. In reality, this was only the first step in a grander process. It took a second great idea to cross the finish line. Once I unclogged the bottleneck by launching my books, all of the previous work paid off. So, don't be discouraged if you don't succeed right away. Your first great idea may be the initial step in a much larger journey.

Growing Your Writing Success

In the next chapter, I share ten of my favorite ideas for increasing writing success. Then, in chapter four, I provide ample opportunities to put these ideas into practice. As you read, I will continue to cheer you on. The positive tone of this book is intentional and is far more than mere fluff. Two years ago, my friend Eric lent me his enthusiasm when I needed it most. I want to give you the same gift Eric gave me. If you are frustrated, discouraged, or feeling down on your luck, understand these feelings will pass.

You are a writer. You have an important message to share, and you are only an idea or two away from your dreams. Regardless of whether it takes one great idea, or multiple ideas stacked together, as long as you persist, you will succeed!

Ideas for Writing Success

If I could send a series of notes back in time to my younger self, I know exactly what I would say. First, I would cheer on the younger me. Because discouragement is a writer's greatest foe, I would encourage him to keep going. A hopeful optimism would be at the forefront of each letter. Looking back, I notice that in my first attempts to write a book, I gave up far too easily.

Next, I would share some basic writing ideas. These ideas are so modest my younger self would likely want to rush past them. Nevertheless, I would share them anyway. As a writing coach, I know that when students try to bypass the foundational principles, it is a good indication I am on the right track. Isn't this how things usually work? The aspiring athlete longs to practice flashy techniques to incite cheers from the crowd. On the other hand, the professional coach knows that refining the basics first is what wins games.

This next section contains ten of the best writing ideas I know. Each one is fundamental and necessary. These ideas are written in letter format, and each one begins with the words, *Dear Writer*. This is because I am writing to you, I am writing to me, and I am writing to everyone who aspires to make a difference in the world.

Even though these letters are brief, don't underestimate their effectiveness. Sometimes success comes from complex ideologies, but most often, it results from a steady application of key principles. So, learn these strategies quickly. Apply them regularly, and you will grow. Remember, one great idea is all it takes to reignite momentum and achieve your writing dreams!

Idea #1
Write Incessantly

Dear Writer,

Start writing! Don't wait for the ideal conditions because they will never come. Instead of convincing yourself that you must learn more first, start now and dive in wholeheartedly. Write incessantly. Writers write, and everything else can be learned along the way.

Years ago, I longed to write a book, but I kept getting stuck. Then I heard two words that changed everything: *writers write!* I took this idea to heart. The next morning, I woke up early, determined not to stress about my bad spelling, poor grammar, lack of artistic style, or the fact that I had absolutely no idea how to publish my book once it was complete. Instead, I brewed a pot of coffee, banished my doubts, and got to work. I did the same thing the next morning and the morning after that.

The simple habit of daily writing was my missing ingredient.

My suggestion is to follow a similar pattern. Wake up early. Set multiple alarms if you must. Better yet, place one alarm close to your bed and one farther away. This way, you have to actually get out of bed to turn them off. Once you are awake, get down to business.

Writers write! This is the writer's single, most important job. Just as speakers speak, musicians play music, and artists paint, the writer's number one priority is to place words on paper. Before practicing this idea, I was an expert at fooling myself. I convinced myself other work was more important. I had thoughts like:

- I need to learn more about writing first. Then I will transcribe my book.
- I need to improve my spelling and grammar before I begin. (Hint: I now know this is what a proofreader is for.)

- I should send out book proposals, find an agent, and build my audience. Then I can begin.

These intrusive thoughts are lies, lies, and more lies. Although the above actions are not wrong, they are problematic when they detract from the real work. For writers, only one thing matters: the writing. Make the phrase "Writers write" your mantra. Repeat this over and over again. First, complete your outline. After that, dive into your messy rough draft. Then go back through your work, writing and revising until the mess transforms into a masterpiece. Writers write, and this is what you must do.

A straightforward strategy for taking action is a game called *Don't Break the Chain*. First, print out a wall calendar for the month. Then, post it near your writing desk. Each day you write, commemorate the day by placing a large red x on the calendar. Your goal is to string together as many x's as possible by writing consistently. Under no circumstances are you to break the chain. While there is nothing magical about this calendar, it is a powerful visual reminder that can help you build momentum fast.

Personally, I am astonished at how gratified I feel each time I place an x on the page. After a small chain of x's accrues, the pressure to keep going is real. For some authors, a tiny dose of accountability is exactly what is needed to grow their writing habit.

Idea #2
Know the Best is Ahead

Dear Writer,

You must keep writing, no matter what. Your very best writing will be accomplished in the days ahead. Yesterday, you may have poured your heart and soul into your work. You might believe what you have written is the best that is in you. Or perhaps you think it is all you have to give. Nevertheless, if you keep writing, there will come a day when you look back on your current work and cringe.

You will think to yourself, *There is so much in this book I could improve upon.* But don't fret. This is a good thing. It means you have honed your craft. As long as you keep pressing forward, I can promise you will grow. This is why I firmly believe your best writing is yet to come.

On the other hand, know there will also be days when you find yourself in a sour mood. It will feel like your best efforts only produce mediocre results. This is an excellent time to remind yourself the best is yet to come. *Maybe I need to write an ordinary book before I can write an extraordinary one,* I thought to myself. There are plenty of days when this thought keeps me moving forward.

Not everything you write will be amazing, and not every bit of writing needs to be. So, determine to lighten up and enjoy the process. Learning to write well is an ongoing journey and not a onetime event. Write daily, and you will experience what Darrin Hardy calls *the compound effect.*[4] Do one set of pushups, and the results are hardly noticeable. Keep this habit up for a week, and you may see a slight change. Stick with your routine for a year, and you will see results.

Determine to hone your skills daily, and new growth will follow. It may not be noticeable at first, but it will come. This is why you must keep going. Your best writing is ahead!

Put this idea into practice by learning to identify and change negative self-talk. When you are discouraged, see if you can detect the specific thoughts running through your head. Then, replace them with one of the following statements,

- My best writing is in front of me. If this book is mediocre, then it puts me one step closer to writing the great book I know I have in me.
- Even though sometimes I feel like an imposter, I am one step ahead of my audience, and this makes me enough of an expert to complete this book.
- Writers write. The fact that I am writing means today is a success.
- Because I practice persistently, my writing is continuing to improve.

Albert Ellis, the founder of Rational Emotive Behavior Therapy, often pointed out that people have an uncanny ability to disturb themselves. He used words like *awfulizing* and *catastrophizing* to describe how people take mole-hill-sized problems and build them up to look like Mt. Everest in their minds.

I wonder if the majority of Ellis's clients were writers, as we certainly have a knack for making problems grander than they are. The next time you get knocked down by feelings of self-doubt, discouragement, or despair, take a deep breath. Remind yourself your current writing is good enough, and your best writing is yet to come. Then, keep pressing forward!

Idea #3
Write for Your Audience

Dear Writer,

Don't just write. Identify your ideal readers and write for them. Now, you may think, *I don't have ideal readers because everyone can benefit from my book.* As a writing coach, I hear this nearly every day. The unfortunate truth is, if you try to write for everyone, then your book is for no one.

If you doubt this, simply look up some of your favorite books and movies online. If they are popular enough, I can practically guarantee there will be a few one-star reviews. Writing for everyone is impossible. No matter how life-changing your book is, no matter how great a writer you become, once your work gets in front of enough eyes, the critics will come.

Elbert Hubbard said, "To avoid criticism, say nothing, do nothing, and be nothing."

Bland ideas are always the least offensive, and the more you try to please everyone, the more uninteresting your book will become. So, do yourself a favor and niche down now.

The best way to avoid critical remarks is to identify your primary audience and write to them. Occasionally, a cynic will find you anyway. When this happens, don't fret. There is little we can do to change someone else's negative attitude, and our books are not for pessimists anyway. Instead, hone in on your ideal audience with laser-like intensity. Doing this will help you develop a passionate following of raving fans who will muffle the occasional naysayer.

Early on, I received a bad rating from someone who wrote, "I didn't order this book." My first thought was, *And I didn't send it to you!* I have no idea how this disparager ended up with a copy of my book, and ultimately, it doesn't matter. My job is to write to my audience. So, instead of stressing over one bad rating, I got back to work.

Happily, that poor review is now lost in a sea of positive voices. The same can be true for your book. Instead of wasting time trying to change a naysayer's mind, get back to work. You have a tribe of fans who are eager to get their hands on your next masterpiece. Turn your attention to them.

In his book *Strengths Finder 2.0*, Author Tom Rath goes against the popular wisdom that we should focus on weaknesses until they become strengths. Instead, he suggests we concentrate on our strengths and develop them to their maximum potential. Tom states, "You cannot be anything you want to be - but you can be a whole lot more of who you already are."[5] Put this wisdom into practice by directing your attention to your primary audience. These are the people who love you for exactly who you are. Doing this will allow you to shine.

Of course, I am not suggesting that we never listen to constructive feedback. Insights from one's primary audience are always beneficial, even if they are challenging to hear. The bottom line is that it is essential to attend to the right people. With an estimated 7.6 billion people on the planet, niching down is easy. To put this idea into action, ask the following questions:

- What does my ideal reader look like?
- Is my book more geared toward men or women?
- Will a younger or older audience relate to my message best? (Try to narrow down your primary audience to an age range of ten years or less.)
- Is my book for singles, adults, or married couples?
- Do my readers have children? If so, how many, and how old are they?
- What faith is my primary reader, and how passionate are they about their beliefs?
- Is my book geared toward intellectuals or readers who prefer everyday English?
- What other books does my primary audience enjoy?

The answer to these questions will give you insights into the demographics and psychographics of your ideal reader. Next, identify someone you know who fits this description. Then, write to that person. This will make your writing warmer and keep you on track.

In his masterpiece *How to Win Friends and Influence People*, Dale Carnegie advises, "Talk in terms of the other person's interests."[6] Writers can modify this to, "Write in terms of your ideal reader's interests." Applying this simple wisdom will keep your readers engaged.

A second simple way to take action is to search through newspapers and magazines for a picture to represent your ideal audience. Preferably, the person in the image will fit the age, gender, and stereotypes of your model reader. Then, cut out the picture and place it on your desk. This will help you keep your reader at the front of your mind.

Finally, know that your book's reach will extend beyond your target audience. Don't worry that you have niched down too far because your ideal readers are by no means your only readers. Instead, they are who you will focus on when you must decide whom to please.

For example, I write for busy parents with young children at home. These parents long to consume useful, life-changing content in small bites. Often, they only have a few minutes to read before a little one tugs on their pant leg, demanding their attention. Because it feels good to finish a book, I intentionally keep my writing short. This allows my primary audience to learn quickly, finish my books, and rack up a series of quick wins.

Fortunately, my audience is not confined to young parents alone. I sometimes receive emails from grandparents who thank me for ideas that help them with their grandkids. Of course, I never reply, "Oh no, you can't read my books because you are not my primary audience." Instead, I thank them for their kind words and celebrate their successes with them.

Know that after you publish your book, your actual audience will expand beyond your ideal audience. In other words, you will end up with the best of both worlds — a broad reach and a passionately engaged tribe. So, start by identifying your ideal readers and write to them.

Idea #4
Identify Your
Writing Style

Dear Writer,

Before writing, it will help to identify your primary writing style. This is also described as finding your voice. Using your natural style makes writing easier and prevents you from sounding like a fraud. Take action by determining which of the following writing personalities fits you best.

The Professor: The Professor is educated and writes as an expert in his field. The Professor typically does not share much of his story, as he is more interested in facts than in forming personal relationships. The Professor's greatest strength is his knowledge of the material. He writes as a legitimate authority in his field.

The Reporter: The Reporter's job is to interview, investigate, and uncover the facts. If you are a reporter, you probably enjoy diving into interviews and events. The Reporter's strengths include connecting with others, drawing out details, examining multiple points of view, and writing from an unbiased perspective.

The Sherpa: The Sherpa are a group of people who lead explorers to the top of Mount Everest. The Sherpa writer's motto is, "I have been where you are. I have been where you want to go, and I can help guide you there." Sherpa writers share personal anecdotes of success and failure. Their superpower is the ability to journey alongside their readers, teach from life experiences, and inspire change.

The Storyteller: The Storyteller is as engaging as they come. Her job is to weave a good tale. For the Storyteller, drawing the reader into the narrative and driving the story forward takes precedence over everything else. The

Storyteller's superpower is her ability to engage readers and incite strong emotions.

The Pastor: The Pastor has a robust moral compass. He writes out of his calling, and his books are typically a passion project. When an aspiring author says, "If my book only reaches one person, it will be worth it," I suspect this person is writing from the Pastor's perspective. The Pastor cares far less about what readers think than any of the other writing styles. The Pastor's superpower is his ability to hone in on values and stay true to them no matter what.

The Rockstar: The Rockstar has a following and knows it. She is not actively seeking new readers because readers are already looking for her. She has an enthusiastic tribe ready to buy her books the moment they are released. The Rockstar's superpower is her ability to be the message. Her tribe longs for more of her, and this is precisely what she provides.

Now it is time to act. Experiment with the different writing styles. Have fun discovering your unique voice. Then, once you find it, embrace it. Decide what kind of writer you are and get consistent. This is how you will shine.

Idea #5
Share You

Dear Writer,

No matter what voice you choose, make your book unique by sharing you. In the Bible, the author of Ecclesiastes states, "There is nothing truly new on earth."[7] Nowhere is this truer than in writing. When was the last time you came across an idea that was 100 percent unique? The truth is, most things worth saying have been said before.

It is estimated that 130 million different books have been printed since the beginning of time. The odds of producing something entirely original is minuscule. This is a reality today's writers face. But don't let the statistics discourage you. Instead, let them motivate you to share more of you.

Although your information may not be completely original, it doesn't have to be. Readers grow slowly, and great ideas sink in over time. Likely, your audience will need to hear the same thoughts presented from multiple perspectives before they take action. This means you have much to add to the conversation. You have a unique viewpoint only you can provide. Therefore, if you want your book to stand apart from the masses, all you must do is share yourself.

Although this is scary at first, don't hold back. Determine to press through your fears. Write about topics dear to your heart. Boldly share your pain and failures, because pain and failure are topics to which everyone can relate. Of course, be sure to share successes with your readers too. Show them simple ways you live out the wisdom you teach.

I often describe intimacy as into-me-see. If you allow readers to glimpse your inner world, then your work is guaranteed to be unique. Put this idea into action by asking the following questions:

- Is my writing too sanitized? Do I make my life appear so unruffled that readers can't relate?
- If so, what rough edges can I write about to assure readers I understand their pain?
- What valuable life lessons have I learned, and what stories best illustrate these points?

In one of my first jobs, I served as a children's pastor in a small church. When the congregation heard that I had moved into my condo with only a few supplies, they generously donated their used pots, pans, and other household items. Because I was young and still learning to cook, I burned a lot of food. Sometimes it took hours of soaking and scrubbing for those pans to come clean.

Years later, I discovered the miracle of nonstick pans. What a time saver! The smooth coating allows charred food to effortlessly slide off. The bottom line is that a smooth, nonstick coating is an immense blessing on cookware. Yet, in relationships, we need rough edges to connect. Our failures, shortcomings, and mistakes help readers to bond with us and cause our message to stick. So, don't be afraid to share both successes and failures when you write.

Lastly, know that being honest does not mean sharing everything. Most often, one or two key stories are enough. To put this idea into practice, imagine your life as a series of snapshots. Carefully search through your mental photo album and share the snapshot that best illustrates your point.

When sharing, remember you are not obligated to provide all of the details. Delivering too much information only confuses readers. Instead, choose your best photograph—the one example that drives your point home. Doing this will make your book unique and allow you to connect like never before!

Idea #6
Add Vitamins and Highlight Pain Pills

Dear Writer,

Every morning my wife, Jenny, and I give our three-year-old daughter, Emmalynn, a multivitamin. We do this because we want her to grow up healthy and strong. The company that makes these vitamins are geniuses. The nutritional supplements come in gummy form, and Emmalyn thinks they are candy.

We give our daughter a multivitamin because Jenny and I believe that years from now, this will make a difference. When writing, it is a good idea to pack your book with vitamins. It is impossible to go wrong by adding long-term value to your readers. So, fill your book with as much wisdom as possible. Just know vitamins alone may not provide enough motivation for readers to buy your book.

The problem with vitamins is they have almost no sense of urgency. When the supplement bottle is empty, Jenny adds them to our running grocery list and picks up a new bottle whenever she has the chance. Although vitamins are good for us, they rarely inspire action.

This is where pain pills come into play. When our three-year-old has an earache, Jenny and I act at once. When a toddler hurts, everyone is miserable. As a result, pain is treated immediately. It doesn't matter if there is an hour wait at the pharmacy. When my children are hurting, I will do whatever it takes to ease their pain.

Now, let's apply this to your book. If readers see your book is packed with vitamins, they may think to themselves:

- *This book looks great! I'm going to wait for my next paycheck and then I'll buy it.*
- *Wow, I need to read this! I'll get it as soon as I finish the other three books I'm reading.*

Of course, readers are easily distracted by the next shiny object—at least I know I am. If potential readers don't buy your book when it is fresh on their mind, there is a good chance they never will. So, in addition to packing your book with vitamins, find a pain point your book relieves, and highlight the relief.

Perhaps your readers struggle with fear, anxiety, or an ongoing frustration. Maybe they long to make a difference in the world but don't know where to start. Perhaps your readers can mentally envision where they want to be but have no idea how to get there. All of these are legitimate pain points which your book can help solve.

In *80/20 Sales and Marketing*,[8] author Perry Marshal describes *The Bleeding Neck Principle*. When people hurt, they will go to great lengths to ease their pain. If your book offers relief, readers will want to hear what you have to say, immediately. Your book is not going back on the shelf.

To put this principle into practice, start by asking the following questions.

- What is my reader's "bleeding neck?"
- How do I offer readers relief from this pain?
- How can I highlight the pain pills in such a way that readers both buy and read my book?

Great places to highlight pain pills include:

- The back cover
- Your book's sales copy
- The introduction
- The beginning of each chapter

In short, pack your book full of vitamins by including plenty of long-term value. Then, highlight the pain pills or the immediate relief your book brings. If you can do these two things, then readers will eagerly buy your books and return to them again and again!

Idea #7
Grease the Chute

Dear Writer,

If you want to keep readers engaged, then turn your book into a greased chute. This simple idea will make your book easy for readers to pick up and difficult for them to put down. When I hear the words *greased chute,* I picture the two-story metal slide at my childhood summer camp. When I was a kid, we campers would sneak disposable, wax-covered cups out of the dining hall and rub the wax onto the slide. This would allow us to zip down at 2x and even 3x speeds. Of course, camp staff would try to prevent us from doing this for our own safety. But it sure was fun!

Similarly, in a greased-chute book, reading feels effortless. Ideally, your audience will lose track of time as they glide through the pages of your book. The greased-chute principle says the goal of your chapter titles is to entice your audience to read the first sentence. The purpose of the first sentence is to compel readers to continue to the second sentence. Likewise, the goal of the first paragraph is to attract readers to the second paragraph. In a greased-chute book, every word counts. Each line is compelling and is written with one's ideal reader in mind.

My favorite strategy for turning a book into a greased chute is to create as many open loops as possible. An open loop is simply an unfulfilled promise. For example, you might write, "Have you ever wanted to write a book but found yourself frustrated instead? Perhaps you sat for hours staring at the dreaded white screen of death because you had no idea what to say next. I have, and I know how painful this feels. In the pages ahead, I will teach you three steps for overcoming writer's block that work for me every time. Hint, one idea is so easy you can accomplish it in your sleep." Then, after broaching the topic, move on without providing a solution. You have now left an open loop. Readers will need to keep reading to find the answer.

The open loop principle works because the human brain longs for resolution. If you let readers know a solution to their problem is approaching, they will keep reading to find it. In this chapter, I am going to model what I teach by leaving an open loop. You can find quick tips for beating writer's block, including one that is so easy that you actually can do it in your sleep, in my book *Ten Quick Wins for Writers*.[9] Typically, I suggest opening and closing loops in the same book. However, in this case, you will have to check out my other book to close the loop.

The key to opening and closing loops is to make a bold promise up front. Let your readers know that you have a solution they need—one that solves their bleeding neck problem. Then, give readers time to get excited and dream about the possibilities.

There are numerous benefits to bringing a bleeding neck problem to your reader's attention and allowing their anticipation to build. Challenges do not arise overnight, and they won't be solved in a matter of minutes. As my old karate instructor used to say, slow to learn also means slow to forget. Open loops allow readers to engage in a transformational process. This not only keeps them interested, but it also helps them learn.

Like a good cup of coffee that takes time to brew, let hope percolate in your reader's minds. There is much wisdom in that old adage: tell your readers what you are going to tell them. Tell them. Then, tell them what you told them. Information that gets reinforced over time has a far greater chance of generating life change.

A successful salesman once told me it takes an average of six offers to the same person to close the deal. I believe it! Personal growth is difficult. Open loops not only make your book a greased chute, but they also allow readers to enter into a process of change. To open a loop, simply make a bold promise to your readers and then wait to deliver that promise.

Some writers open lots of loops in the introduction and then close them, one by one, throughout the book. Other writers open a loop, close it, and then immediately open another. Just be sure every promise is fulfilled by the end of the book. Opening and closing loops will transform your book into a greased chute, where readers slide from one paragraph to the next with ease!

Idea #8
Learn from
Running Partners

Dear Writer,

Some authors may tell you to know your competition, but I suggest learning from your running partners instead. What if competition is a myth? In writing, I don't believe you have opponents. Instead, you have running partners who can help you succeed if you decide to learn from them.

Three years ago, I wrote *131 Creative Conversations for Couples,* a book which has sold well over 11,000 copies. This was followed by a series of eight more books, all with the number 131 in the title. As you might imagine, I am often asked, "Jed, why did you choose the number 131?" The answer is simple. When researching my running partners, I discovered the most popular conversation starter books had 101 creative questions. I wanted to offer readers a little more, and the number 131 felt right.

Back then, I would have referred to the other conversation starter books as my competitors. However, today I know better. When my wife, Jenny, and I were dating, we went through a conversation starter book ourselves. We had a blast working through the questions in coffee shops, on road trips, and during long walks on the beach. When we reached the end of the first book I asked, "What conversation starter book should we work through next?"

As an avid reader, I know book lovers devour numerous volumes on the same topic. As a self-help book addict, I freely admit to buying several books with similar themes because I want multiple perspectives. This means other conversation starter books are not competitors but running partners.

Of course, I prefer that readers purchase my book first, which is why I examine what other authors are doing. Then, I strive to give a little extra. I want to stand apart from the crowd. Nevertheless, should readers buy my running partner's book first, I want them to think, *But I am going to buy Jed's book next.*

Mentally shifting your view of other authors makes a big difference in several ways. First, many digital platforms have an "also bought" section. When marketing my book, one goal is to end up on my running partner's also-bought page. Thus, my fellow authors help me succeed. Both of us have similar audiences who are interested in the same topics, so teaming up is natural. Ray Crock, the founder of McDonald's, said, "None of us is as good as all of us." Viewing equivalent writers as running partners will keep you open to working together, which will help both of you reach more readers.

This is called an abundance mindset, and this type of thinking is in direct opposition to the scarcity mentality. The scarcity mindset says, "If someone buys my competitor's book, then they will not purchase mine." Thinking like this puts you at odds with other writers in your genre. On the other hand, the abundance mentality says, "After a reader finishes my running partner's book, they are certain to want mine next!" This type of thinking creates a bond between you and your fellow authors.

I personally know one independent author who earned a place on a highly competitive bestseller list by teaming up with fellow writers. Each author wrote one chapter in the book, and all of the writers promoted the book to their tribes. Through their combined efforts, thousands of books were sold. When you transform your competition into running partners and friends, the possibilities are endless. Not only will you sell more books, but you will also have more fun along the way!

Idea #9
Surprise and Delight
by Giving More

Dear Writer,

To the best of my knowledge, no reader ever said, "Please stop! You are adding too much value to my life." Thus, if readers feel like they are drinking water out of a firehose, you are on the right track. When writing, make it your aim to give a little more than everyone else. Although we touched on this idea in the last chapter, overdelivering is so important it warrants a section of its own.

Recently I heard a fitness expert proclaim he never ends on an even number of repetitions. For example, when doing pushups, the numbers ten, fifty, or one hundred are natural stopping points. However, this trainer suggests that doing eleven, fifty-one, or even a hundred and one iterations is far better.

Although one extra pushup will not drastically increase your muscle mass, it does create a powerful mindset shift. The additional pushup is a reminder you can always give more. So, make it your aim to overdeliver by providing extra value.

In today's highly competitive world, you don't need to be miles ahead to win. A slight edge is all it takes. Runners win races by being a fraction of a second faster. Similarly, you can win over new readers by giving more than other writers. In the company I work for, this is called *surprise and delight*, and every employee is responsible for putting this principle into practice.

A desire to surprise and delight readers is what prompted me to include 131 conversation starters in my book, as opposed to the standard 101. Despite its short length, this book is one of my all-time bestsellers, and this is no mistake. After researching other conversation starter books, I noticed most of them contained little information outside of the conversation starters. As a result, I decided to surprise and delight readers by including a chapter with practical strategies for connecting with their loved ones.

The key to surprising and delighting readers is providing an unexpected bonus. However, don't stress yourself out. The bonus does not need to be colossal. To accomplish this, first identify your core running partners. Then, ask yourself, *How can I give more? What bonus can I provide that will surprise and delight my audience?* Putting this idea into action will motivate readers to buy your book first!

Idea #10
Reject Perfectionism and Ship Your Book

Dear Writer,

Suggesting you finish your book and publish it is hardly a novel idea. Nevertheless, if you are a perfectionist, like me, then shipping your work is much easier said than done. At the end of every book I write, I always think to myself, *This is OK, but I wish I could say it better.* Then, I write and revise, write and revise, and write and revise some more.

According to the *Strength's Finders 2.0* assessment,[10] I am a maximizer. This means I love taking things that are good and making them great. The problem is, in my mind, my books are never good enough. I always think to myself, *If I go over this one more time, I can make it better.* This is great for the 2nd, 3rd, and even the 4th draft. However, by the time the

20th revision rolls around, I know I have issues.

Today, I try to follow the advice given in Lewis Carroll's masterpiece, *Alice's Adventures in Wonderland*, "Begin at the beginning... and go on till you come to the end: then stop."[11] This quote reminds me my book does not have to be perfect, nor does it need to be the final word on the subject. Our world changes fast, and new insights are being made continually. Not only is it impossible to include every idea in our books, attempting to do so will overwhelm readers.

Personally, I love reaching the end of a book. This brings me a feeling of success. In fact, I enjoy this so much I would rather read multiple books, each covering one small aspect of a broad topic, than one book which includes everything. So, don't be afraid to niche down and write an inch wide and a mile deep. Instead of adding new material to your current book, consider incorporating new insights you gain during the revision process into your next book. I suggest always keeping a file for future books close at hand. This way, when a fresh idea pops into your head, you can easily file it away and get back to the work at hand.

Once your book is written and edited, take a deep breath. Remind yourself that done is better than perfect. Now is the time to break up with perfectionism and ship your book. Remember, your book reflects who you are at this moment. Not every reader wants advice from someone who is highly successful.

A few years ago, a fellow blogger and I bemoaned how difficult it was to find insights from bloggers who were one or two steps ahead of us. Tracking down articles by massively successful bloggers was easy. Yet, their advice was so advanced it was out of touch with our reality. The point is some readers want to hear what you have to say in the stage you are in right now. They don't need you to grow your expertise first and doing so might be a turnoff.

Because of this, don't wait to ship your book. Once you are finished, declare your work "Done!" and courageously publish. In writing, nothing is guaranteed. There are books I poured my heart and soul into that remain hidden treasures on the digital shelves. On the other hand, books I wrote on a whim—merely because I thought they would be fun to write—have steadily increasing sales and a broad readership.

Before publishing, I like to view my book as an experiment. Like the mad scientist holding a tube of elixir in each hand, the experiment of publishing my book is going to generate new information. The mad scientist smiles maniacally because he knows once the beakers are mixed, he might uncover a secret that turns lead into gold. On the other hand, the concoction could explode in his face. However, no matter what happens, the scientist will be wiser as a result, and this is why mad scientists smile. No matter what happens, they win!

Whether your book is a raging success, a dismal failure, or somewhere in between, one thing is sure. After publishing your book, you will be more knowledgeable than you are now. So, don't get stuck on the hamster wheel of revisions. Say what you need to say, edit your messy rough draft, get your work proofed, and then ship your masterpiece.

Creating a stress-free shipping process allows you to move on to your next book. Successful writers write, publish, promote, and repeat. They learn from reader feedback and grow from the process of writing many, many books. So, don't allow perfectionistic tendencies to prevent you from sharing your book with the world. Instead, start at the beginning. Say what you need to say. When you reach the end, stop. Lastly, break up with perfectionism, and share your masterpiece with the world!

Bonus: Idea #11
Do It All Over Again

Dear Writer,

I know… I know… This book is titled *Ten Great Ideas for Authors,* and this is idea number eleven. The beautiful thing about writing is that it's an art and a science. In art, it is perfectly acceptable to occasionally bend a rule. However, please know that I am bending rules for a reason. In addition to teaching new ideas, I also want to model the principles I teach. I hope this bonus chapter comes as a surprise and a delight.

.

After you publish your book, there is just one primary task left—decide on your next book and repeat the process. Remember, writers write. Of course, you want to take a moment to celebrate, but afterward, it is time to get back to work.

If you want to build a book-based business, then one book is a good start, but it is not enough. According to the 80/20 rule, also known as the Pareto Principle, 80 percent of book sales will come from 20 percent of the books we write. This means that if your first book is not a smashing success, there is no need to fret. That book is simply not a part of your 20 percent that sells well. However, because it is published, you are now one step closer to writing your next 20 percent book.

Ever since learning about the 80/20 rule, I began noticing this principle everywhere. Roughly 80 percent of my speaking engagements come from 20 percent of my books. Happily, this often includes books that are outside of my bestsellers. In other words, books that do not generate massive sales may create advantages in other areas.

Understanding this vital principle is energizing. Regardless of what happens after you publish, keep going. You are a writer, and writers write. Act on this powerful idea by seamlessly transitioning to your next book shortly after you publish.

These eleven simple writing ideas have served me well. Although much more could be said about the writing process, all it takes is one great idea to make massive strides. If I could send a sequence of letters back in time, this is precisely what I would say. In fact, I would end my messages like this…

Dear Writer,

Perhaps you find yourself wondering, *Can writing and publishing truly be this easy?* The answer is *Of course not!* There is, indeed, much more to learn. Yet, all it takes is one great idea, and as you know, ideas are of little value until they are acted upon. I have no doubt that these eleven ideas are enough to get your momentum going.

Now is the time to come full circle. Writers write. Learning about writing is essential. Nevertheless, it is the writing itself that moves the needle the most. In this book, my letters are intentionally short because I want to leave you with plenty of time to act. Now that you understand these ideas, it is time to put them into practice. This is exactly what the next chapter is about. In the next section, you will find 131 creative writing prompts to help you share yourself and get your message into the world.

There is nothing magical about these writing prompts, other than the fact they encourage you to get started. Whether you use these ideas in a social media post, a blog post, or as a subsection in a book, these writing prompts will help you apply the great ideas you know.

Write, publish, promote, and repeat. Do this over and over again. This gritty work is necessary for growth. Notice which pieces of writing fall flat and which ones resonate with readers. Get pragmatic by pinpointing what works and giving your audience more of what they want.

Then, repurpose and expand your best content. Turning a popular social media post into a longer blog post, and a blog post into a book is perfectly acceptable. Because change takes time, readers will benefit from hearing your message again and again.

Now it is time for the real work to begin. Use the creative writing prompts in the next chapter to get started. Know that I am cheering you on and wish you happy writing!

131 Writing Prompts
for Action Takers

Your story is an ongoing event and not a onetime process. You are an ever-growing work in progress. Philippians 1:6 says, "For I am sure of this very thing, that the one who began a good work in you will perfect it until the day of Christ Jesus." This passage declares that God is nowhere near being finished with you and me yet. Instead, He is leading us down an ongoing path of transformation.

This is excellent news for writers. Because your story is continuously expanding, you never need to be stuck. You can always share more of your unfolding adventure. Right now, you have everything you need for fresh, engaging content. This chapter will help you add value to others by sharing your story, one piece at a time. It contains 131 creative ideas to help you get started.

Personal Growth Writing Prompts

Creative Writing Prompt #1

If I could travel back in time, three pieces of advice I would give my younger self are…

Creative Writing Prompt #2

My favorite self-development book is… This book influenced my life by…

Creative Writing Prompt #3

The three most important life lessons I learned this year are…

Creative Writing Prompt #4

Three leadership quotes that influenced my life are… These quotes matter because…

Creative Writing Prompt #5

When I feel stressed, I practice healthy self-care by doing these three things…

Creative Writing Prompt #6

My most significant personal development challenges are… I am striving to grow in these areas by…

Creative Writing Prompt #7

Three life skills I want to pass on to my children are… I am passionate about these skills because…

Creative Writing Prompt #8

Three things I do to successfully resolve disagreements include…

Creative Writing Prompt #9

Five ways I add joy to my life are… You can add joy to your life, too, by…

Creative Writing Prompt #10

The biggest mistakes I made in my personal growth journey were… Here is what I learned from my mistakes.

Faith-Based Writing Prompts

Creative Writing Prompt #11

I am a follower of Jesus Christ because…

Creative Writing Prompt #12

A time in my life when I saw God answer prayer was when…

Creative Writing Prompt #13

My favorite Bible verse is… Three ways this passage of Scripture adds value to my life include…

Creative Writing Prompt #14

Three things I do to keep my faith strong on a daily basis are…

Creative Writing Prompt #15

The most important thing God taught me this year is…

Creative Writing Prompt #16

One piece of spiritual advice I would offer to new Christians is… This advice is essential because…

Creative Writing Prompt #17

My favorite Bible story is… Three things this story taught me include…

Creative Writing Prompt #18

A time when my faith was tested happened when… Some things I learned from this experience are…

Creative Writing Prompt #19

When it is hard to trust God, I keep following Him by doing these three things…

Creative Writing Prompt #20

A fellow Christ-follower I admire is… The qualities I most appreciate in this person are…

Family and Parenting Writing Prompts

Creative Writing Prompt #21

One of my greatest parenting successes happened when…

Creative Writing Prompt #22

A recent parenting fail I learned from occurred when… My biggest takeaway is…

Creative Writing Prompt #23

Some of the best parenting decisions my parents made were… Their parenting helped me grow because…

Creative Writing Prompt #24

Our grandest family adventure happened when… Some practical tips for stirring up more adventure in our family include…

Creative Writing Prompt #25

Some important values I want to instill in my children are...

Creative Writing Prompt #26

Our family demonstrates God's grace at home by...

Creative Writing Prompt #27

Three pieces of parenting wisdom that I gleaned from my dad are...

Creative Writing Prompt #28

Three things my mom taught me about parenting include...

Creative Writing Prompt #29

A book that positively influenced my parenting is... I am a better parent for following this advice because...

Creative Writing Prompt #30

The best advice I have to offer new parents is to...

Creative Writing Prompt #31

Three positive discipline strategies that work in our home include...

Creative Writing Prompt #32

List 4-5 of your favorite parenting quotes. Then, write about why each quote is important to you or how it influenced your parenting.

Creative Writing Prompt #33

My biggest parenting challenges this year are... Three things I am doing to overcome these obstacles are...

Creative Writing Prompt #34

Three films every family should watch together are... Some valuable life lessons that families can learn from these movies include...

Creative Writing Prompt #35

My favorite ways to build happy memories with my children include...

Creative Writing Prompt #36

If I could travel back in time and parent differently, three things I would change are... The reasons I would make these changes include...

Creative Writing Prompt #37

A straightforward piece of advice for resolving family conflicts is...

Creative Writing Prompt #38

When parenting is stressful, we use these strategies to recharge...

Creative Writing Prompt #39

Some unique activities our family uses to connect are...

Creative Writing Prompt #40

Growing up, my happiest childhood memory was... This moment was so meaningful to me because...

Friendship
Writing Prompts

Creative Writing Prompt #41

The best advice I ever gave to a friend was… Here is how following this wisdom can help you grow…

Creative Writing Prompt #42

My must-have qualities in a good friend are… You can foster each of these qualities in your relationships by following these steps…

Creative Writing Prompt #43

The biggest argument I ever had happened when… If I could travel back in time and do things differently, I would change…

Creative Writing Prompt #44

The most beautiful thing a friend ever did for me was… Here is why this act of kindness mattered so much…

Creative Writing Prompt #45

The best advice I ever received from a friend was… This wisdom changed my life because…

Creative Writing Prompt #46

Three things I do to keep friendships healthy now that I am married include…

Creative Writing Prompt #47

Five things I do to develop healthy and encouraging relationships online are…

Creative Writing Prompt #48

My favorite books on friendship are… Some fundamental principles I learned from them include…

Creative Writing Prompt #49

I am building into the lives of my friends this month by… You can follow my example by…

Creative Writing Prompt #50

The biggest life lessons I have gleaned from my friends are…

Writing Prompts
for Writers

Creative Writing Prompt #51

If I were to restart my blog, three things I would do differently include…

Creative Writing Prompt #52

Five things I learned in my first year of writing are… (Or the second year of writing, etc.).

Creative Writing Prompt #53

When life gets busy, I balance writing and family life by…

Creative Writing Prompt #54

My favorite things about writing are…Three things I do to keep the joy alive when writing gets frustrating include…

Creative Writing Prompt #55

Five strategies I use to write consistently are…

Creative Writing Prompt #56

The story behind why I started writing is… Some reasons you may want to consider starting a blog or writing a book include…

Creative Writing Prompt #57

Three blogs that I think everyone should read include… These blogs matter because…

Be sure to tell each blogger they are included in your post so they can share your awesome writing with their tribe. Most bloggers I know are honored and happily promote posts that highlight their remarkable work. It is a win-win situation!

Creative Writing Prompt #58

Three strategies I use to grow my audience are… So far, the results of using these strategies are…

Creative Writing Prompt #59

My writing goals for this month include…

Creative Writing Prompt #60

My writing theme for the year is… I chose this theme because…

Creative Writing Prompt #61

The most valuable piece of writing/blogging advice I ever received is… Here is how this advice transformed me into a better writer/blogger…

Creative Writing Prompt #62

Five things I do to balance work, family, and writing include…

Creative Writing Prompt #63

If I were only able to write one blog post or book this year, but it was guaranteed to be seen worldwide, I would write on this topic… because…

Creative Writing Prompt #64

My favorite writing tools are… You can find the tools I use on these sites…

Creative Writing Prompt #65

My three biggest writing mistakes have been… Here is what I learned from them…

Creative Writing Prompt #66

My reason for writing is… Here is how you can help me share this important message…

Creative Writing Prompt #67

My writing manifesto—or the wrong in the world that I am picking a fight with—is…

Creative Writing Prompt #68

My biggest writing failure happened when… This is what I gleaned from the experience…

Creative Writing Prompt #69

My most significant writing success happened when… This experience taught me…

Creative Writing Prompt #70

Three steps I take to stay motivated in my writing include...

Personal
Writing Prompts

Creative Writing Prompt #71

Ten things you probably don't know about me are…

Creative Writing Prompt #72

My five favorite smartphone apps include… Each of these apps enhances my life in the following ways…

Creative Writing Prompt #73

My top three all-time favorite books are… Here is why I consider each book a must-read…

Creative Writing Prompt #74

My personal goals for this year include…

Creative Writing Prompt #75

A typical day in my life looks like…

Creative Writing Prompt #76

My writing setup and routine is… (Be sure to include a picture or video of your desk and author tools.)

Creative Writing Prompt #77

My weekly exercise routine looks like… Here is how I am improving my physical health this year…

Creative Writing Prompt #78

To stay mentally sharp, I… Here is how you can get started with an intellectual growth plan…

Creative Writing Prompt #79

A time I was stuck in life (stuck in my career, personal growth, poor eating habits, etc.) was when… Here is how I got unstuck and how you can gain momentum too...

Creative Writing Prompt #80

My favorite self-care strategies are… I know self-care is vital because…

Relationship Writing Prompts

Creative Writing Prompt #81

Three of my favorite dates with my husband, wife, or partner include…

Creative Writing Prompt #82

Five of the best ways my spouse shows me he or she cares are…

Creative Writing Prompt #83

A couple I admire is…The qualities I most appreciate about this couple include… I am integrating these qualities into my own relationship by…

Creative Writing Prompt #84

The most important advice I have for newly married couples is…

Creative Writing Prompt #85

My favorite book on marriage is… Some of my greatest takeaways from this book include…

Creative Writing Prompt #86

A recent marriage success happened when… Here is how you can have similar successes in your marriage…

Creative Writing Prompt #87

A recent marriage fail happened when… Here is what I learned from it and what I plan to do differently in the future…

Creative Writing Prompt #88

A recent marriage conflict arose when… Here is how my spouse and worked together to resolve it…

Creative Writing Prompt #89

Three of my favorite marriage quotes are… Here are the reasons these quotes are so powerful…

Creative Writing Prompt #90

The most significant lessons I have learned about marriage so far are…

Get Organized Writing Prompts

Creative Writing Prompt #91

My must-have apps for staying organized are...

Creative Writing Prompt #92

Three things I do to help our busy family manage our schedules are…

Creative Writing Prompt #93

Three things I do to be more productive at home are…

Creative Writing Prompt #94

When time is tight, here is how I continue to create happy memories with my children…

Creative Writing Prompt #95

Three ways my spouse and I keep our marriage healthy when life is busy include…

Creative Writing Prompt #96

My greatest organizational challenge is… Here are the practical steps I am taking to get more organized this month…

Creative Writing Prompt #97

My must-have organizational household supplies include…

Creative Writing Prompt #98

Three tricks I use to help my children stay organized include…

Creative Writing Prompt #99

The single most important lesson for getting organized is…

Creative Writing Prompt #100

To get organized, first I had to break these lousy habits …

Life Lesson
Writing Prompts

Creative Writing Prompt #101

The most essential life lesson I learned this month is…

Creative Writing Prompt #102

My all-time favorite movie is… Here is what this movie taught me about myself…

Creative Writing Prompt #103

I am currently reading… My biggest takeaway from this book is…

Creative Writing Prompt #104

If I could have one do-over this month, I would change…

Creative Writing Prompt #105

An unexpected life lesson I recently learned happened when…

Creative Writing Prompt #106

A saying, quote, or Scripture that I strive to live by is… These words help me to be a better person because…

Creative Writing Prompt #107

When life is difficult, three things I do to keep myself going include…

Creative Writing Prompt #108

The most important personal growth lesson my parents taught me is…

Creative Writing Prompt #109

Three work and career-related lessons I want to pass on to my children include…

Creative Writing Prompt #110

The most crucial positive parenting lessons I know include…

Just for Fun
Writing Prompts

Creative Writing Prompt #111

One of my all-time happiest memories is…

Creative Writing Prompt #112

The most disastrous date I ever went on happened when… A lesson I learned from this experience was…

Creative Writing Prompt #113

The story of how I met my husband/wife is…

Creative Writing Prompt #114

The superhero I can most relate to is… If I had this hero's powers, I would make the world a better place by…

Creative Writing Prompt #115

If I was stranded on a deserted island, three things I would bring with me are…

Creative Writing Prompt #116

The best vacation I ever took was… Here is what made my vacation so awesome…

Creative Writing Prompt #117

A recent happy memory is…

Creative Writing Prompt #118

The top five places in the world I would like to visit are… The first thing I would do in each location is…

Creative Writing Prompt #119

My summer bucket list is… Or do a bucket list (a list of fun, must-do activities) for each season of the year.

Creative Writing Prompt #120

My top ten favorite clean jokes are…
For added fun, have your friends, family or children help you compile this list.

Social Media Writing Prompts

Creative Writing Prompt #121

My favorite social media sites include… Here is what I appreciate about each of them…

Creative Writing Prompt #122

My must-have social-media apps for relieving stress and goofing off include …

Creative Writing Prompt #123

Five ways I use social media to build a stronger relationship with my spouse are…

Creative Writing Prompt #124

Three strategies I use to keep my kids safe online are…

Creative Writing Prompt #125

Five excellent online tools I use to help my children grow include...

Creative Writing Prompt #126

Three ways I am teaching my children to use social media responsibly are…

Creative Writing Prompt #127

What I say when I talk to my children about online safety is… I think parents need to start having these conversations with their kids when…

Creative Writing Prompt #128

Three things I do to unplug and build face-to-face relationships include…

Creative Writing Prompt #129

Social media etiquette I think everyone should follow is… Here are how these strategies make cyberspace a better place for everyone…

Creative Writing Prompt #130

Warning: avoid this social-media advice at your own risk! Social media lessons I learned the hard way include…

Creative Writing Prompt #131

Creative ideas for my next ten blog posts, books, or social media posts include…

Motivation for Massive Writing Action

One Saturday morning, when I was five years old, I was overcome by a sense of urgency to do something that mattered. I had no idea what I would do, but I knew I needed to act.

I scurried through the house, gathering as many art supplies as I could find. I piled them on our dining room table and began to think. A short time later, my mom walked by and asked what I was doing. I replied, "Mom, I want to make something that does something," with as much enthusiasm as I could muster.

This was my childish way of saying, "I want to make a difference in the world." My mom replied, "Honey, that's nice." However, I could tell she didn't understand. Because I wanted my mom to connect with my newfound passion, I repeated this statement two more times. However, repeating myself only confused her. When I noticed the look of bewilderment on her face, tears streamed down my cheeks.

Looking back, it is no surprise I became a pastor, then a therapist, and now an author. The desire to "make something that does something" has never gone away. When I was in seminary, we were told the average church has approximately fifty members. *Wow!* I thought to myself, *If I could grow a church to one hundred attendees, I would be at twice the national average.* This knowledge both excited and frustrated me. The thought of reaching one hundred people was exhilarating. However, it also did not feel like enough.

When my books began reaching one hundred readers a month, then one hundred readers a week, and eventually, one hundred readers a day, I knew I was on to something. Finally, I am making something that does something. For me, writing books has opened the door to Narnia. Books allow me to work from home, do what I love, and connect with more people than I dreamed possible.

So first of all, thank you for purchasing this book. You have helped me fulfill a childhood dream. Know that I have sought to pack as much valuable information into this short work as possible. Similar to my other books, I aimed to keep each chapter brief, easy to understand, and hyper-actionable. I genuinely want you to spend the majority of your time writing. After all, this is the real work we writers do.

You are reading this book because you have a valuable message to share. Like my five-year-old self, you may also long to "make something that does something." I know that getting started can be frightening. The timing is probably not right. More than likely, you are too busy to write as much as you would like. Maybe financially it does not make sense. Perhaps you know far less about writing and publishing than you would prefer. If any of these hindrances apply to you, then congratulations, you are normal. Looking back on my journey, I now understand the best time to start writing was yesterday, and the second-best time to begin is right now.

Perhaps you wonder how I know so much about the struggles I write about. I know because this is nearly every writer's journey, and it was most certainly mine. Over the past five years,

Jenny and I have moved four times — including a major transition from San Diego to Minnesota. Shortly after starting to write seriously, Jenny and I had two more kids. Recently, we opened our home to two foster children. This brings our family's grand total up to nine — me, Jenny, six children, and one hyperactive cat.

When I started writing, I had no inkling what I was getting into. Self-doubt kicked into high gear. The annoying chatterbox in my head incessantly reminded me of the teacher assistant job I didn't get hired for because my spelling and grammar were that atrocious. Yet, I pressed forward anyway.

I connected with self-published friends over coffee, and I learned from them. After our third daughter was born, I held her in one arm, balanced my laptop on my knees, and pecked out the next lines in my book with my free hand. When my initial books generated only a few sales, I smiled over the positive feedback I received, learned from each experience, and kept going.

The good news is that my story does not need to be your story. You may knock it out of the park with your first book. Or, you may slowly build momentum over time. Ultimately, what matters is giving everything you have to offer. You are a writer, and it is time to share your message with the world. I believe if you do the work, if you write, publish, promote, and press forward, eventually, amazing things will happen.

I have learned it is nearly impossible to predict what those fantastic things will be. Some books generate many sales. Others lead to deep, lasting friendships. Several opened doors to speaking engagements, seminars, webinars, podcasts, online courses, writing for a popular magazine, and even to a new career as a writing coach.

I am living proof that writing is an adventure and publishing a book can open the door to Narnia. Where will writing lead you? There is only one way to find out, and that is to dive in. So, if now is not a good time to start, my suggestion is to begin anyway. Write your book. Publish it. Share your message with the world.

Most of all, fulfill your calling—the one present since childhood. Make something that does something. I, for one, am glad I did.

I am cheering you on and wish you much success in your writing adventure!

Sincerely, Jed Jurchenko

Endnotes

1. Kiyosaki Robert T, *Rich Dad Poor Dad,* Plata Publishing, April 11, 2017.

2. Publishing Perspectives, *200 Million Americans Want to Publish Books, But Can They? May 26, 2011* https://publishingperspectives.com/2011/05/200-million-americans-want-to-publish-books/

3. Tyler Eric, *The Best Advice So Far*, CreateSpace Independent Publishing Platform, May 8, 2015.

4. Hardy Darrin, *The Compound Effect*, Vanguard Press, November 1, 2011.

5. Rath Tom, *Strengths Finder 2.0*, Gallup Press; 1 edition, September 1, 2013.

6. Carnegie Dale, *How to Win Friends and Influence People*, Simon & Schuster, August 24, 2010.

7. Ecclesiastes 1:9b. Scripture quoted by permission. All scripture quotations, unless otherwise indicated, are taken from the NET Bible® copyright ©1996-2016 by Biblical Studies Press, L.L.C. All rights reserved.

8. Marshall Perry, 80/20 Sales and Marketing, Entrepreneur Press, July 22, 2013.

9. Jurchenko Jed, *Ten Quick Wins for Writers,* independently published, February 20, 2019.

10. Rath Tom, *Strengths Finder 2.0*, Gallup Press; 1 edition, September 1, 2013.

11. Carroll Lewis, *Alice's Adventures in Wonderland*, Jovian Press (November 26, 2017)

About the Author

Jed is passionate about helping people live happy, healthy, more-connected lives by having better conversations! He is a husband, father of four girls, a psychology professor, success coach, speaker, therapist, and writer.

Jed graduated from Southern California Seminary with a Master of Divinity and returned to complete a second master's degree in psychology. In his free time, Jed enjoys hiking, walking on the beach, reading, and spending time with his incredible family.

Continue the Conversation

If you enjoyed this book, I would love it if you would leave a review. Your feedback is an enormous encouragement to me, and it helps books like this one get noticed. It only takes a minute, and every review is much appreciated. Oh, and please feel free to stay in touch too!

Email: jed@coffeeshopconversations.com

Twitter: @jjurchenko

Facebook: Coffee Shop Conversations

Blog: www.CoffeeShopConversations.com

Thumbs Up
or Thumbs Down

Thank you for purchasing this book!

I would love to hear from you! Your feedback not only helps me grow as a writer but also helps me to get books into the hands of those who need them most. Online reviews are one of the most significant ways independent authors like me connect with new readers.

If you loved the book, could you please share your experience? Leaving feedback is as easy as answering any of these questions:

- What did you like about the book?

- What is your most valuable takeaway from this book?
- What have you done differently or what will you do differently because of what you have read?
- To whom would you recommend this book?

Of course, I am looking for honest reviews, so if you have a minute to share your experience, good or bad, please consider leaving a review!

I look forward to hearing from you!

Sincerely, Jed Jurchenko

More Books by Jed

This book and other books by Jed are available at www.Amazon.com.

Transform from stuck and frustrated to writing with ease! This motivational book for writers is based on time-tested principles from psychology. It will help you to ignite your creativity, write steadily, and publish your book.

Ten Quick Wins for Writers

More Books by Jed

These creative conversation starters will inspire your kids to pause their electronics, grow their social skills, and develop lifelong relationships!

This book is for children and tweens who desire to build face-to-face connections and everyone who wants to help their kids connect in an increasingly disconnected world. Get your kids talking with this activity book the entire family will enjoy.

131 Conversations That Engage Kids

Made in the USA
Middletown, DE
22 February 2020